FINANCIAL FOUNDATIONS

A TEENAGER'S GUIDE TO MASTERING MONEY

RUTH PETERS

COPYRIGHT

Copyright © 2023. Ruth Peters

All rights reserved

TABLE OF CONTENT

COPYRIGHT

TABLE OF CONTENT

INTRODUCTION

SETTING FINANCIAL GOALS

UNDERSTANDING BUDGETING

SAVINGS AND INVESTMENTS

UNDERSTANDING CREDIT

BANKING AND FINANCIAL SERVICES

MAKING MONEY

CASE STUDIES AND REAL-LIFE EXAMPLES

CONCLUSION

INTRODUCTION

Welcome to "Financial Foundations: A Teenager's Guide to Mastering Money!" In this book, we embark on an exciting journey together—one that will equip you with the knowledge and skills to navigate the complex world of finances and set you on a path to financial success.

Understanding money is one of the most important skills you can acquire at this transforming stage of your life. Being a teenager comes with its own set of obstacles and responsibilities. Building a strong foundation in financial literacy now will provide you the knowledge and skills you need to make wise choices, establish worthwhile goals, and pave the road for a safe and prosperous future.

In this book, we'll look at a variety of financial issues and break them down into principles that teenagers can understand easily. This book will give you the fundamental building blocks required to make wise financial decisions, regardless of your level of experience in the financial world.

We'll start by recognizing the significance of establishing financial goals. You'll get the ability to fulfill your dreams by learning how to define your aspirations and develop a plan to get there. After that, we'll dive into the fundamentals of budgeting, showing you how to control your income, keep track of your costs, and develop responsible spending practices.

The book's main themes will be investing and saving. We'll talk about the importance of saving money, the different kinds of savings accounts, and introduce you to the fascinating world of investments. You'll discover how to manage your finances effectively, comprehend risk and return, and choose investments wisely.

Another crucial component of financial literacy is understanding credit. We'll explain credit scores, show you how to use credit cards responsibly, and show you how to steer clear of financial traps. We'll also go into the realm of banking and finance, demystifying the many account kinds, internet banking, and exposing you to the fundamentals of loans and mortgages.

However, this book also discusses how to make money, so it's not simply about making money. We'll delve into the world of side hustles and entrepreneurship to give you the skills you need to land a job, launch your own side hustle, and handle your finances wisely.

An essential talent in today's environment is consumer awareness. We'll talk about the tricks and strategies used in advertising, show you how to make wise purchasing decisions, and provide you the knowledge and resources to spot and stay away from fraud and scams.

We'll discuss the ideas of financial independence and long-term planning last. You'll discover the value of developing a career plan, the significance of a college education and student loans, and even how to begin making retirement plans—a long-term objective that might seem far off but is essential to guaranteeing a pleasant and secure future.

You'll find useful advice, examples from real-world situations to help you learn more throughout this book. It is intended to be your dependable friend, giving you the confidence and knowledge you need to make sound financial decisions.

Remember that your financial future will be shaped by the decisions you make now. So let's start this adventure together and lay a solid financial foundation that will benefit you in the future. Are you willing to embark on this path toward your financial future? Let's start now.

THE PURPOSE OF FINANCIAL LITERACY

I want to underline the value of financial education and why it is so important for your future success as you approach adulthood. Understanding how to handle money and make educated decisions becomes crucial in a world full of complex financial issues. You can successfully navigate the world of personal finance with the knowledge and skills you gain through financial education. The necessity of financial education for you as a teen will be discussed.

The main benefit of financial education is that it gives you the power to take charge of your financial future. It gives you the resources you need to make decisions that are in line with your objectives and desires. You get a greater grasp of your financial options by learning about budgeting, saving, and investing. You have the power to set worthwhile objectives, make practical budgets, and make deliberate choices regarding your spending and saving. Your ability to avoid frequent traps and make wise financial decisions that create the groundwork for a prosperous future is empowered by financial knowledge.

Financial education also teaches you the value of money and the significance of practicing sound financial management. Understanding how to handle your income becomes increasingly important as you start earning money from side jobs or receiving allowances. You gain a sense of financial responsibility through learning about budgeting and financial planning. You develop good spending practices, learn to distinguish between necessities and wants, and steer clear of the temptation to make impulsive or wasteful purchases. You develop an understanding of the work involved in earning money and the significance of handling it carefully as a result of financial education.

Understanding credit and debt is a key component of financial education. You can make wise judgments if you have knowledge of credit scores, how to use credit cards responsibly, and the dangers of debt. You may appropriately manage the credit and debt world by being aware of these ideas, preventing future financial difficulties. Your ability to establish and maintain a solid credit history, which is necessary for tasks like renting an apartment or getting a loan, will be improved by financial education.

Additionally, receiving a financial education helps you develop an entrepreneurial perspective. It challenges you to use your imagination, spot opportunities, and acquire the abilities needed to launch and run your own firm. Your potential for self-employment and financial independence is unlocked by embracing an entrepreneurial mindset. It gives you the resources to control your own future and build money according to your own standards.

Financial education teaches you the value of long-term planning and investing in addition to urgent financial concerns. You have the ability to make smart judgments when you comprehend various investment options, risk management, and the significance of compound growth over time. You can start investing early and enjoy the advantages of long-term wealth creation by planning for the future. You may cultivate a mindset that emphasizes long-term goals and gets you ready for a stable financial future by learning about finances.

Additionally, financial education gives you the critical thinking abilities you need to successfully navigate the consumer culture. Financial knowledge gives you the power to make wise purchasing decisions in a world full of commercials and marketing strategies designed to influence your selections. It assists you in determining the genuine worth and requirement of things, making cost-effective choices, and avoiding the pitfalls of misleading marketing techniques. You can make decisions that are in line with your principles and financial stability by learning to be a discriminating consumer.

Finally, financial knowledge helps you develop resilience and the ability to face unforeseen financial issues. It highlights the significance of emergency savings, insurance, and risk control. You may build the resilience required to weather financial storms and preserve stability in the face of unpredictability by comprehending these ideas. Your ability to adapt and overcome financial challenges that may develop during your life is enhanced by financial education.

Your future will be shaped by your financial education, dear adolescent. It equips you with useful knowledge, abilities, and a mindset that enable you to make wise choices, seize chances, and reach your objectives. By making an investment in your financial education today, you can lay a strong foundation for a profitable future while gaining the confidence and skills necessary to negotiate the complexity of personal finance. You will be well on your path to financial success and freedom if you seize the chance to learn about finances.

Give yourself the knowledge and abilities you need to make wise decisions and ensure a prosperous future. Start your road toward financial education today, and you'll benefit in the long run.

CHAPTER 1

SETTING FINANCIAL GOALS

You must understand the importance of creating financial objectives as you begin your adult life. Understanding and establishing your financial ambitions when you are young can have a profound impact on your future, even though it may seem like a far-off idea.

You can manage your money with greater clarity and purpose if you have financial goals. Without goals, it's simple to become caught up in a loop of pointless spending and lack of attention to one's finances. By setting objectives, you build a road map that directs your financial choices and inspires you to work for particular accomplishments.

Goals act as strong motivators that help you achieve your desired financial results. They provide you a sense of direction and aid in setting your priorities. You are more likely to make deliberate decisions that support your goals when you have a clear goal in mind, whether it's saving for a dream vacation, getting your first automobile, or paying for your education. Setting goals helps you avoid distractions that can impede your financial growth and keeps you focused on what matters most to you.

You can develop a long-term vision for your life by setting financial goals. They nudge you to examine your financial future and to look beyond the here and now. You can take proactive actions today that will benefit your future self by picturing the life you want to live and the financial security you seek. Setting objectives enables you to lay a solid basis for the future, whether it's retirement savings or constructing a financial safety net.

When faced with financial options, goals serve as filters for choice. They offer a framework for determining if a specific spending or investment is in line with your targeted results. By pondering the question, "Will this purchase move me closer to my objectives?You can choose carefully and refrain from making rash or unneeded purchases. Setting goals gives you the focus and direction you need to make wise financial decisions that support your long-term aims.

Setting financial goals offers a number of benefits, one of which is the ability to track your progress. Goals serve as standards by which you can measure your financial progress. You may keep track of your progress toward your goals and recognize major victories along the way. This sensation of achievement strengthens your dedication to your objectives and inspires you to keep moving in the direction of financial success.

Setting financial goals is important, but it's also critical to keep in mind that these objectives are not fixed in stone. Your goals may need to be adjusted when your circumstances in life change. Financial objectives should be flexible and adaptable in order to account for unanticipated circumstances or shifting priorities. Accept the chance to periodically review your objectives and make changes to reflect your changing needs and desires.

Setting financial goals gives you the power to improve your financial life and take charge of your financial destiny. By establishing your goals, you may manage your finances with greater focus, drive, and purpose.

Financial objectives provide you a long-term perspective, direct your choices, and let you track your advancement over time. Keep in mind that creating objectives is a continuous process that allows for flexibility and improvement. Accept the power of objectives and start down the path to financial achievement. You get closer to realizing your dreams with each step you take.

MID-TERM AND SHORT-TERM GOALS

It's critical to comprehend the significance of setting both short-term and medium-term financial goals as you navigate the realm of personal finance. These shorter-term goals serve as stepping stones towards your longer-term aims, whereas long-term goals offer a vision for the future.

SHORT-TERM GOALS

Financial objectives that are set for the near future, or within a year, usually concentrate on pressing requirements and priorities. These objectives can frequently be swiftly attained and are generally measurable. Let's explore why it's crucial for youngsters like you to make short-term financial goals

One significant short-term goals is to start an emergency fund. It entails saving a modest amount of your salary to save for unforeseen costs like medical bills or auto repairs. You build a financial safety net that gives you peace of mind and defends you against unanticipated financial problems by constantly saving for an emergency fund.

Setting a goal to pay off any outstanding debts is a sensible short-term target if you have any. Whether it's a loan or credit card balance, paying off these debts early prevents interest from building up and frees up your cash for future initiatives. Making a strategy to pay off debts on time exemplifies sound money management and prepares the road for a more secure financial future.

You can enjoy the gratification of accomplishing concrete results within a realistic timeframe by setting a short-term goal to save for a specific item, such as a smartphone, concert ticket, or gaming console. You can enjoy the thing you want while developing responsible saving habits if you routinely set aside a percentage of your salary.

MID-TERM GOALS

Medium-term financial goals bridge the gap between short-term objectives and long-term aspirations, often lasting one to five years. These objectives call for greater preparation and commitment, but they are still doable in a fair amount of time. Let's talk about why setting medium-term financial goals is important for young people like you.

Saving for College:

One of the most important medium-term financial objectives is to invest in your education. Whether you want to pursue specialized training, vocational school, or college, saving for your education costs shows that you are responsible and have good planning skills. You can support your educational endeavors and lessen dependency on student loans by setting a medium-term goal to save for tuition fees, books, or living expenses.

Setting up a Travel Fund

If you want to plan and save for fascinating experiences, creating a travel fund as a medium-term objective will help you fulfill your desire to discover new places and cultures. Saving for travel allows you to expand your horizons while developing financial discipline and budgeting skills, whether it's a road trip with friends or an international experience.

Putting Money Into Future Goals:

Setting medium-term investing objectives might still be helpful even though long-term goals may be more suited for long-term investments. To invest a percentage of your income in stocks, bonds, or mutual funds, think about learning about the fundamental investment alternatives and choosing a goal. By making medium-term investments, you may watch your money increase while laying the groundwork for future dreams like financing higher education or the purchase of a car.

In conclusion, setting short- and long-term financial goals will help you on your way to financial success. Short-term objectives take care of pressing issues like putting together an emergency fund, paying off debts, and setting aside money for certain expenditures. On the other hand, medium-term goals cover a wider range of objectives like setting up a travel fund, saving for schooling, and investing for the future. You build financial discipline, foster responsible habits, and build a strong basis for your long-term desires by creating and completing these goals. Always keep in mind that reaching your short- and medium-term objectives will help you get closer to the future you want for yourself.

LONG-TERM FINANCIAL GOALS

Understanding the significance of creating long-term financial objectives is essential as you set out on your path to financial independence. Long-term objectives act as a compass to help you make financial decisions and shape your future, while short-term and medium-term goals provide you instant direction and concentration. We'll talk about the importance of long-term financial goals and how they can help you live a successful and happy life.

The Strength of Vision

Long-term financial objectives help you visualize and create the life you want. They encompass aspirations that may span several years or even decades, going beyond the present requirements and desires. By outlining your long-term objectives, you may envision your financial future and give your financial journey a sense of direction. This vision serves as a beacon, encouraging you to make decisions and perform activities that are in line with your long-term goals.

Increasing financial stability

The chance to create long-term financial security is one of the main advantages of adopting long-term financial goals. Long-term objectives demand regular effort and discipline over a protracted period, whether they are saving for a down payment on a home, starting a business, or building a retirement fund. You progressively lay a solid foundation for financial security by making deliberate decisions and directing resources toward your long-term objectives. You have the peace of mind and freedom to follow your passions and aspirations thanks to this security.

Making Use of Compounding's Power:

You can take advantage of compounding by setting long-term financial goals. Your money has the potential to expand massively over time if you make sensible investments and give it time to mature. The longer you hold an investment, whether it be in stocks, bonds, or retirement funds, the higher the potential returns. You may take advantage of compounding and position yourself for significant financial development in the future by starting early and staying dedicated to your long-term investing goals.

Making Retirement Plans:

Planning for retirement, which may seem far off but is essential for financial stability, is a common step in setting long-term financial goals. Planning for retirement makes sure you have the resources to live comfortably and pursue your hobbies in your later years. By saving a percentage of your income for retirement, you give yourself the gift of financial independence and freedom when you are no longer able to rely on a steady stream of income. The more time you have to accumulate a sizeable nest egg, the earlier you should begin planning for retirement.

Realizing Individual Dreams and Goals:

Long-term financial objectives also help you fulfill your own hopes and dreams. These objectives frequently call for time, money, and financial security, whether they are related to starting your own business, touring the world, seeking further education, or helping philanthropic causes. Setting long-term objectives helps you build a plan for making your ambitions come true. You learn the financial restraint, strategic reasoning, and resiliency required to get beyond challenges and realize your goals.

Adaptability and Flexibility:

Although long-term objectives give you a feeling of direction, keep in mind that life is full of surprises and changes. Financial long-term objectives should be flexible and responsive to changing conditions and priorities. It's important to regularly examine and reassess your long-term goals as you move along in your financial journey, making adjustments as required. This adaptability enables you to respond to potential new possibilities while maintaining alignment with your beliefs.

Finally, my dear adolescent, establishing long-term financial objectives is a discipline that empowers you to control your financial future. By setting long-term goals and working toward them, you may create financial security, take advantage of compound interest, prepare for retirement, and make your dreams come true. Always keep in mind that reaching long-term objectives necessitates consistency, dedication, and adaptability. Accept the strength of long-term financial objectives and start down the road to a rich and happy life.

"SMART" FINANCIAL GOALS

Understanding the idea of SMART financial goals is essential as you set out on your path to financial independence. The letters SMART, which stand for specific, measurable, attainable, relevant, and time-bound, are an acronym. By creating a framework for your financial future through the use of SMART financial goals, you can build focused and actionable financial plans. Let's talk about why it's important to develop SMART financial goals and how you can use this strategy to improve your personal financial situation.

Specific goals

It's critical to be detailed when defining financial objectives so that you can reach them. Be more specific as opposed to having a general goal like "save money." For instance, you can specify that you want to save

$500 over the following six months for a new laptop. You can more easily develop a plan to reach your objective by giving clarity and concentration by outlining the precise quantity and purpose of your goal.

Measurable goals

Progress monitoring is essential for keeping you on track and evaluating your accomplishments. You can quantify your progress and assess if you are headed in the correct direction by setting attainable financial goals. For example, instead of saying "pay off debt," make a measurable objective like "pay off $1,000 of credit card debt within the next three months." In this way, you can evaluate your progress and recognize accomplishments as you approach your goal.

Attainable goals

While it's great to have lofty dreams, it's also crucial to create objectives that are both attainable and practical in order to stay motivated and avoid disappointment. When establishing your goals, take into account your present income, expenses, and financial condition. Set smaller, more manageable objectives that you can constantly strive toward as opposed to lofty ones that can demoralize you. Always keep in mind that attaining lesser goals will inspire you to take on bigger ones in the future.

Relevant goals

It's critical to make sure your financial objectives are in line with your overall financial aspirations and values when you set them. Why is achieving this objective important to you?" and "How does it affect my overall financial health? It will give you a feeling of purpose and strengthen your dedication to attaining your goals if you align them with your beliefs and long-term vision. If you value education, for instance, having a goal to save a certain amount for college tuition would be appropriate.

Time-Bound goals

Your sense of urgency will increase and you'll be better able to stay focused if you give your financial goals a deadline. Set deadlines for each of your goals rather than keeping them open-ended. For instance, you can give yourself six months to reach your goal of saving $2,000 for a summer vacation. A deadline encourages you to start acting, create a calendar, and divide your goal into more manageable tasks.

Set SMART financial goals for yourself, dear adolescent, since this will help you take charge of your financial destiny. You provide yourself a clear road map for success by making sure your goals are Specific, Measurable, Achievable, Relevant, and Time-bound. Always keep in mind that your goals should be suited to your particular situation, aspirations, and beliefs. You may make steady progress, maintain motivation, and confidently move toward a prosperous financial future by setting SMART financial objectives.

Check out the story of this young champ

Alex is a young man living in a small town of Oakville. Alex had always dreamed of becoming financially successful and building a comfortable life for himself. He knew that it would require careful planning and strategic goal setting to achieve his desired life, for himself and his family. Inspired by the SMART principle, Alex set out on a journey to achieve financial success.

Alex's goal was to save enough money to start his own business. He wanted to open a bakery, as he had always been passionate about baking and saw it as an opportunity to turn his hobby into a profitable venture. He envisioned a bakery that would delight the taste buds of his community and become a go-to spot for delicious pastries and bread.

To make his dream a reality, Alex began by setting measurable goals. He calculated the amount of money needed to start the bakery, including equipment, ingredients, and rental costs, it was estimated at $30,000. The goal was clear, Alex needs to raise $30,000 within the next three years.

Alex knew that achieving this goal would require discipline and a realistic approach, he analyzed his current financial situation, taking into account his income from his full-time and part-time jobs, his monthly expenses and other anticipated expenses. With careful budgeting, he determined that he could save approximately $750 per month towards his bakery business.

Alex focused on making his goal achievable. He researched cost-effective ways to acquire baking equipment and supplies, finding second-hand options and negotiating favorable deals, he also explored different ways to increase his income, taking on additional part-time job during weekends and at night.

Throughout the journey, Alex ensured that his goals remained relevant to his passion for baking and the long-term vision of owning a successful bakery. He constantly reminded himself of why he was pursuing this dream, envisioning the joy it would bring to customers with the delectable treats.

As time went by, Alex encountered obstacles and challenges. There were moments when doubts crept in, there were months he couldn't meet up to the savings, and some months he made more than the $750, he was so determined and resilient. He knew that setbacks were part of the process, and he learned from other people's experiences making adjustments and staying focused on his goal.

Finally, after three years and four months of hard work, dedication, and disciplined saving, Alex achieved his financial goal. With $30,000 in the bakery fund, he was ready to turn his dream into a reality. He found the perfect location for his bakery, purchased high-quality equipment, and hired a small team of passionate bakers to bring his vision to life.

The grand opening of Alex's bakery was a resounding success. People from all over town flocked to taste the delicious pastries and experience the warm and inviting atmosphere. Word quickly spread about the exceptional quality and service, and the bakery became a beloved community spot.

Through the power of SMART goal setting, Alex not only achieved financial success but also found fulfillment and happiness in doing what he loved. The bakery thrived, providing him with a stable income and a sense of pride in his accomplishments.

CHAPTER 2

UNDERSTANDING BUDGETING

One of the most important skills you can learn as you travel the path to financial independence is budgeting. Making informed judgments about how much money you earn, how much you spend, and how much money you save can be accomplished through the process of budgeting.

Everyone should learn how to manage their finances, including teenagers. You may start earning money, getting allowances, or having financial obligations as a teen. Early budgeting education and practice will position you for a future of financial security. Let's talk about the value of budgeting and how it may make your life better.

Teenagers who use a budget can become self-sufficient in their finances. You gain control over your finances and prevent overspending by making a budget. It enables you to set spending priorities, divide up funds for various needs, and put money aside for the future. You become more self-reliant and less reliant on others by managing your finances.

Also, learning to budget early on can help you create sound financial practices that will serve you well in the future. You may increase your awareness of where your money is going by setting spending restrictions and keeping track of your expenses. This routine fosters self-control and discourages impulse buying. You will improve your ability to differentiate between necessities and wants and make wise financial decisions.

Setting and achieving financial objectives is made possible through budgeting. A budget can help you direct money toward your goals, whether they are paying for college, a car, or a dream vacation. The likelihood of accomplishing your goals increases when you plan ahead and save money consistently. You can modify your spending patterns to match your long-term goals by using a budget.

Furthermore, one of budgeting's biggest advantages is its capacity to assist you in avoiding needless debt and financial hardship. You are less likely to overspend or rack up debt when you keep track of your spending and make a financial plan. You lessen your chance of running into financial trouble by living within your means. You can cover your necessary expenses and have a safety net for unforeseen circumstances if your budget is effectively managed.

Developing Financial Management Skills: Budgeting gives you the tools you need to manage your finances effectively. You gain the ability to organize your spending, make wise choices, and take a long-term view of your financial situation. These abilities go beyond budgeting and can be used in a variety of areas of life, including investing, starting a business, and personal finance. You build a solid basis for future financial success by mastering budgeting.

Finally, budgeting is a vital skill that teens should pick up early. Understanding the value of budgeting can help you become financially independent, form sound spending habits, make plans for the future, stay out of debt and out of worry about money, and learn important money management techniques. You position yourself for a financially secure and stable future by taking charge of your finances right away. Accept budgeting as a tool for success and take pleasure in the advantages it offers your life.

UNDERSTANDING INCOME AND EXPENSES

INCOME

You might start making money as a teen from allowances, part-time work, or other sources. Understanding the idea of income and its importance in your life is crucial.

The term "income" refers to the money you make or get from various sources. It can come from a job, such as pay or salary, or from other sources, such as stipends, presents, or investments. Your ability to manage your spending and put money aside for the future is based on your income, which is the cornerstone of your financial health.

Let's examine the different forms of income:

Earned Income: This includes any compensation you receive for performing work, such as through freelancing work, internships, or part-time jobs. Your time, abilities, and effort directly contribute to your earned revenue.

Passive Income: Income generated with little to no active effort on your side is referred to as passive income. Investments, rental properties, royalties, and commercial endeavors are all potential sources. In the long run, passive income can give you financial security and freedom by allowing your money to work for you.

Portfolio Income: Income from investments in stocks, bonds, mutual funds, or other financial instruments is referred to as a portfolio. When you sell investments for a profit, it comes from capital gains, dividends, and interest payments.

EXPENSES

As an adolescent, it's critical to comprehend expenses and how they affect your financial situation. Your purchases of numerous items, services, and activities are referred to as expenses. You can create appropriate spending habits that will serve you well throughout your life by becoming aware of your expenses and managing them sensibly. Let's examine the various expense categories.

Fixed Expenses: Fixed expenses are ongoing costs that are generally constant from month to month. Rent or mortgage payments, insurance premiums, subscription fees, and loan repayments are a few examples. Usually necessary, fixed costs should be given top priority in your budget.

Variable Costs: Variable costs vary from month to month and are influenced by your lifestyle and preferences. These can include household goods, leisure activities, dining out, clothes, transportation, and toiletries. For a business to be in balance, variable costs must be monitored and managed.

Discretionary Expenses: These out-of-pocket costs frequently reflect personal preferences and leisure activities and are not necessary. Vacations, pastimes, entertainment, and opulent purchases might all fall under this category. Although luxuries can make life more enjoyable, it's crucial to set priorities and invest your money sensibly.

Understanding the importance of budgeting is essential for managing your income and expenses as a teen. Making educated judgments, controlling your spending, and achieving your goals are all made possible with the use of a budget, which is an effective tool.

The following are some ways that budgeting can keep your income and expenses in balance

Organizing and Planning Your Finances: Budgeting enables you to efficiently plan and organize your finances. You can divide your money among several expense categories, such as needs, savings, and discretionary spending, by making a budget. This enables you to prioritize your debts and make sure your money is being used effectively.

Budgeting helps you become more financially savvy by making you aware of your income and expenses. You can clearly comprehend where and how your money is being spent by keeping track of your income and expenses. Your ability to make adjustments, spot areas of overspending, and decide on your financial priorities is empowered by this insight.

Managing Your Income: Setting up a budget is essential to wisely managing your income. It aids in distributing your money to pay for necessary costs like housing, utilities, transportation, and education. You can work towards achieving future objectives like paying for college, traveling, or starting a business by designating a percentage of your salary for savings and investing. Making a budget also guarantees that you have adequate cash on hand to handle unforeseen costs or emergencies.

Managing Your Expenses: Budgeting helps you manage your spending and stay out of debt. You can find areas where you can make savings and changes by setting spending caps in each category. By differentiating between needs and wants and making wise decisions about how to spend your money, it promotes responsible spending. You may stop making impulsive purchases and put your financial security first by using a budget.

Building Financial Discipline: Budgeting helps you develop financial discipline, a crucial ability for successfully managing your income and expenses. By sticking to a budget, you can improve your ability to limit your spending, gain self-discipline, and fend off the need to overspend. It motivates you to stick to your budget, stay out of debt, and lay a strong foundation for your financial future.

Getting There: Budgeting serves as a road map for reaching your financial objectives. Budgeting assists you in allocating money towards these goals methodically by helping you create precise goals, such as saving for a car or education. It helps you stay motivated and accountable by giving you a clear schedule and plan for achieving your goals. By creating a budget, you can make sure that your income matches your long-term goals.

Adapting to Changing Situations: Budgeting enables you to adjust to shifting financial and social conditions. Your ability to make essential adjustments as your income and expenses change is facilitated by having a budget in place. Budgeting enables you to efficiently reallocate cash in the event of a fall in income or unanticipated expenses.

In managing your income and expenses as a teenager, budgeting is crucial. It gives you a path to financial success, encourages wise spending, and aids in goal achievement. You develop financial awareness, develop discipline, and have the ability to make wise financial decisions by organizing, planning, and controlling your resources through budgeting. Accept budgeting as a useful tool for managing your income and expenses and laying the groundwork for a prosperous and satisfying future.

Check out the monthly budget of a 15 year old teenager

Income

- Monthly allowance: $100
- Wages from part-time job: $120 monthly
- Total monthly income: $220

Expenses

- Transportation: $20
- Food: $60

- Entertainment (movies, games, outings, etc.): $30
- Personal care items (toiletries, etc.): $10
- Other expenses (subscription, etc.): $10
- Savings and future goals: $50
- Total monthly expenses: $180

From the above budget, Dan, a 15 year old teenager earns $220 and expends $180 monthly. Following his budget strictly, Dan has additional $40 monthly for unexpected expenses and emergencies.

This is a sample budget, it could be adjusted based on individual needs, financial goals and circumstances. Regularly reviewing and updating the budget will help you stay on track with your financial responsibilities and aspirations.

GOOD LUCK CHAMP!

CHAPTER 3

SAVINGS AND INVESTMENTS

Building a strong financial foundation as a teen requires mastering the ideas of investing and saving. Savings and investing both need careful money management, but they serve different objectives and have different features. To better grasp these crucial components of personal finance, let's examine the definitions of savings and investments, point out their commonalities, and go through their contrasts.

Savings are the process of putting some of your money away for the future. It entails depositing funds into an account for saves or keeping them in a secure location for future accumulation. Savings are mostly used to achieve short-term financial objectives, financial security, and emergency reserves. Investing entails utilizing your money to fund projects or purchases with the hope of earning a profit over time. The purpose of investments is to increase your wealth and accomplish long-term financial goals. Investments, in contrast to savings, include some risk and demand thought.

Let's examine the significance of saving for you.

The significance of saving money as a teen cannot be overemphasized. Early savings habits provide the groundwork for future success in terms of achieving financial security, independence, and objectives.

Saving money serves as a first line of defense and safety net against unforeseen financial difficulties. Because there are so many unknowns in life, having savings enables you to handle emergencies and unforeseen costs without relying on others or building up debt. Saving money can help you feel more secure financially and give you peace of mind because you'll know you have money to fall back on in an emergency.

Saving money also gives you the ability to become financially independent. It provides you the independence to make decisions and work toward your goals without continually needing financial assistance from others. Saving money enables you to begin developing your own financial resources, reducing your dependence on your parents or legal guardians. This independence encourages responsibility, self-assurance, and a sense of success.

For long-term objectives to be met, saving money is necessary. Savings give the crucial financial foundation to make goals come true, whether they be for paying for further education, launching a business, or purchasing a home. Regular savings will help you build up the necessary funds over time, preventing future financial stress or excessive borrowing. Early saving maximizes the growth of your savings by allowing the power of compound interest to work in your favor.

Saving money also teaches self-control and wise financial management. It teaches you how to tell the difference between necessities and wants, make thoughtful financial decisions, and stay away from impulsive purchases. Saving calls for self-control, self-restraint, and the capacity to postpone satisfaction. You create a strong financial foundation that will serve you well throughout your lives by cultivating these traits early on.

Additionally, as life is full of unforeseen circumstances, having funds guarantees that you are ready for crises. Having a financial cushion enables you to manage these obstacles without experiencing extreme financial hardships, whether it be an unexpected auto repair, medical expenditure, or job loss. Saving money offers peace of mind and lowers stress by serving as a safety net during trying times.

You're encouraged to acquire financial literacy and awareness through saving money. It provides access to education on spending plans, financial investments, interest rates, and other financial ideas. You receive practical experience in money management, goal-setting, and money-related decision-making by actively engaging in saving. You gain useful life skills from this knowledge that are necessary for your success in the future.

Finally, you should make saving money a habit for the sake of your personal financial security. It grants freedom, financial security, and the capacity to realize long-term objectives. Saving teaches discipline, promotes fiscal responsibility, and gets you ready for unforeseen crises. Early savings position you for financial freedom in the future, enabling you to follow your goals and face the uncertainties of life with assurance. Beginning to save at a young age is never too late, and the rewards will last well into adulthood.

It's crucial to start cultivating wise saving practices while still a teen. Teenagers might consider the following assortment of savings options:

1. Basic Savings Account: The most popular and simple option is a basic savings account. It makes it simple to deposit and withdraw money and is often provided by banks or credit unions. Look for accounts with

reasonable or no fees and an interest rate that is competitive. Simple savings accounts are appropriate for general saving, emergency cash, and short-term saving objectives.

2. High-Yield Savings Account: Compared to standard savings accounts, high-yield savings accounts pay greater interest rates. These accounts are frequently offered by financial institutions or internet banks. Teenagers who wish to enhance the growth of their money with higher interest rates can consider high-yield savings accounts. They might be an excellent choice for long-term savings or achieving particular financial objectives.

3. Student Savings Account: A few banks provide accounts just for students. These accounts frequently offer extra advantages like no monthly fees, greater interest rates, or special privileges for students. Teenagers may find student savings accounts to be a fantastic option because they offer a personalized banking experience and help students develop their financial knowledge.

4. Certificate of Deposit (CD): CDs are time-limited savings products with greater interest rates than standard savings accounts. With a CD, you make a deposit of a specific sum for a predetermined amount of time, usually from a few months to a few years. For longer-term savings objectives when you don't require rapid access to the money, CDs are appropriate. Remember that there could be fees associated with withdrawing money prior to the maturity date.

5. Peer-to-Peer Lending: Platforms for peer-to-peer lending link people who want to borrow money with those who want to lend. Some platforms let you invest your money by making interest-bearing loans to other people. Teenagers who have a higher risk tolerance and are interested in learning about alternative financial alternatives may find this option appealing. Before choosing peer-to-peer lending, it's vital to do your homework and comprehend the hazards.

When choosing a savings option, keep in mind to take into account elements like fees, accessibility, minimum balance requirements, and interest rates. Setting up a budget and setting up precise savings objectives will help you figure out how much money you can set aside each month for saves. You may lay a solid financial foundation for the future by starting early and maintaining a consistent savings routine. Don't be afraid to ask for advice from your parents, legal guardians, or financial professionals who can help you choose the best savings choice for your needs as a teen.

INVESTMENT

For someone your age, investing might seem like a far-off idea, but realizing its significance can significantly affect your financial destiny. Let's discuss what investment is and why it's important for young people like you.

Investing is the act of utilizing your money to buy things or start businesses in the hopes of making money over time. It entails investing your money in methods that could increase and expand your wealth. Saving money is important, but investing elevates your financial journey by utilizing the power of compounding and assisting you in reaching your long-term objectives.

Here are some explanations as to why you should consider investing.

Wealth Building: Investing offers the chance to build wealth over time. You might be able to get a better return on your money by investing it in assets like stocks, bonds, real estate, or businesses as opposed to keeping it in a savings account. Younger investors have a longer time horizon for their assets to grow and compound, which increases their likelihood of achieving financial independence in the future.

Investing enables you to become financially independent more quickly. You can develop additional income streams that work for you passively by making wise investment decisions. This income may give you financial security and freedom, enabling you to follow your interests, launch a business, or exercise more influence over your life decisions.

Beat Inflation: Over time, the prices of goods and services increase gradually, causing inflation. If you merely store your money without making any investments, inflation may cause it to lose some of its purchasing power. By investing, you can increase your money's true value and exceed inflation, protecting its purchasing power.

Learn about the Financial Markets: Investing gives you the chance to get to know the stock, bond, and other investment markets. Having information and skills in this area as a teen can assist you in being financially literate and in making decisions that will benefit you throughout your life. You'll learn about economic trends, corporate operations, and the value of diversification in risk management.

Long-Term Objectives: Investments are essential to accomplishing long-term financial objectives. Investing can assist you in accumulating the money required to realize your goals, whether they be to save for a home, a college education, or a comfortable retirement. By getting started as soon as possible, you give your investments more time to grow, improving your chances of success.

It's critical to remember that investing entails risk. Investment values are subject to change, and there is always a chance of financial loss. It is essential to do your homework, comprehend the investments you select, diversify your holdings, and seek advice from knowledgeable people or financial experts.

Keep in mind that you have time on your side as a teenager, which is a big benefit when it comes to investing. The first step is to educate yourself on the many investing options available, such as equities, bonds, mutual funds, and exchange-traded funds (ETFs). If you have money in savings that you won't need right away, think about investing it. As you become older, you can learn more about investing and progressively set aside more money for investments.

The road of investing calls for endurance, self-control, and a long-term outlook. You may position yourself for a safe and profitable future by getting started early and continuing to do so. Accept investing's power, and you'll see your money increase over time.

RISKS AND RETURN ON INVESTMENT

Understanding the connection between risk and return is crucial when making investments. In order to increase profits, investing entails assuming a certain amount of risk. Let's investigate this idea in more detail.

RISK

Risk is the chance that you could lose all or part of the money you invested. All investments involve some level of risk, and the risk involved with various investment options varies. It's important to realize that bigger potential gains frequently include higher dangers.

Over time, the value of investments may fluctuate. Some investments, like stocks, might be more volatile than others, which means their prices can change dramatically over a short period of time. Bonds are one type of investment that tends to be more reliable but still carries some risk. You can evaluate the risk involved in various investing opportunities by being aware of their volatility.

The idea of diversification is to spread your investments over several asset classes, industries, and geographical areas. The danger of putting all of your eggs in one basket is diminished by diversification. Other investments may help to offset losses if one performs poorly. Diversification is a powerful risk management tactic that can produce more consistent outcomes.

Every individual has a unique risk tolerance, which is the degree of risk they are ready to accept. A person's risk tolerance is influenced by factors like financial goals, time horizon, and personal circumstances. It is crucial to assess your risk tolerance and make investments in line with it. If you have a longer investing horizon, you may be more willing to make riskier investments because you will have more time to recover.

RETURNS

Your assets' profits or gains are referred to as returns. The prospective returns on various investment options differ. Generally speaking, higher-risk investments have a greater chance of yielding a profit than lower-risk investments. It is essential to look at an investment option's past performance in order to gauge its potential returns. Past performance, however, does not ensure future results. It is just one factor to take into account when evaluating an investment. Over the long term, returns are frequently felt. Your assets will have more time to multiply and grow if you invest for a longer time frame. You may benefit from the power of compounding, which can greatly enhance your returns over time, by getting started early and exercising patience.

It's critical to strike the ideal balance between risk and return. Even though bigger profits can be alluring, they frequently involve more risk. To make investment decisions that are in line with your comfort zone while still having the potential to generate significant returns, it's critical to consider your risk tolerance and financial objectives.

Keep in mind that risk and returns are inextricably related. Finding the right balance for your financial objectives, risk tolerance, and time horizon is crucial. To properly manage risk, make sure to educate yourself about various investing possibilities, get guidance from financial experts, and diversify your holdings.

The journey of investing calls for serious thought and constant observation. Understanding how risk and returns are related will help you make wise investment choices and work toward your long-term financial objectives.

You have a number of fundamental investment options to think about as a teen. Here are some typical investment alternatives for teenagers, though availability and suitability may differ depending on your age and location:

Stocks: Investing in stocks entails purchasing ownership interests in publicly listed businesses. You might think about making investments as a teen in individual stocks or through diversified investment vehicles like exchange-traded funds (ETFs) or mutual funds that maintain a portfolio of equities.

Bonds: To raise money, governments, towns, and corporations issue bonds, which are debt instruments. When you buy bonds, you are essentially making a fixed-term loan to the issuer in exchange for recurrent interest payments and the return of the principle at maturity. Bonds often have lower returns than stocks but lower risks than stocks. For teenagers, Treasury bonds or corporate bonds might be a good choice.

Mutual Funds: To invest in a wide portfolio of stocks, bonds, or other assets, mutual funds aggregate money from several participants. Funds are managed by professionals. Teenagers who want to invest in a variety of assets without having to choose individual investments might choose mutual funds since they offer diversity and are a handy substitute.

Exchange-Traded Funds (ETFs): Similar to mutual funds, ETFs are traded on stock exchanges just like individual stocks. They offer diversification within a particular index or sector. Since ETFs sometimes have lower expense ratios than mutual funds and let investors buy and sell shares at any time during the trading day, they may be a desirable alternative for adolescents.

Index Funds: An exchange-traded fund or mutual fund that attempts to mimic the performance of a particular market index, such as the S&P 500, is known as an index fund. In addition to offering wide market exposure, they also keep their expense ratios low. For teenagers looking for a simple and affordable way to participate in the market as a whole, index funds can be a great solution.

Education Savings: An education savings account, such as a 529 plan (in the United States), might be a useful investment choice if you want to pursue higher education. These accounts offer tax benefits when putting money down for eligible educational costs. Long-term education savings can be encouraged by the tax-free growth of contributions to these accounts.

Prior to investing, it's crucial to investigate and comprehend each investment option, including the risks involved, potential returns, fees, and any limitations imposed by law or your age. Getting advice from your parents, legal guardians, or financial experts can help you understand the situation better and make decisions about your investments that are based on your own needs.

Keep in mind that investing carries risks, so it's critical to establish your financial objectives, risk tolerance, and time horizon up front. Your financial future, both as a teenager and later in life, can benefit from getting started early and maintaining a steady investment schedule.

CHAPTER 4

UNDERSTANDING CREDIT

Credit is a crucial financial term to understand as you begin to navigate the realm of personal finance. It refers to the capacity to borrow money or gain access to products and services on the condition that you repay the borrowed amount at a later date, often with interest. Credit may be a beneficial tool when used appropriately, but it's critical to understand how it works and the hazards that come with it. Let's start with the fundamentals of credit:

Types of Credit

Individuals can obtain numerous sorts of credit, including:

•Credit cards: Credit cards allow you to make purchases up to a certain credit limit. You must refund the amount spent, either in full by the due date or in minimum payments while interest is accruing on the remaining balance.

•Loan: There are various types of loans, such as school loans, auto loans, and personal loans. When you take out a loan, you are given a lump sum of money that you must back in installments over a set length of time, plus interest.

•Store Credit: Some stores provide credit accounts that allow you to make purchases on credit in their store only. These accounts frequently include additional financing choices or reward schemes.

Building Credit History

Credit plays a significant role in building your credit history. Your credit history is a record of how you've managed credit in the past, including your payment history, amounts owed, and length of credit history. Building a positive credit history is important as it can affect your ability to obtain future credit and the interest rates you may be offered. To build credit, consider these steps:

- Open a Bank Account: Begin by establishing a banking relationship and demonstrating financial responsibility by creating a bank account in your name.

- Ask a Parent or Guardian to Add You as an Authorized User: You can ask a parent or guardian to add you as an authorized user on their credit card. By having your name attached with their account, you can build credit. Ascertain if the primary cardholder has a strong credit history and manages credit responsibly.

- Apply for a Student Credit Card: Some financial institutions provide credit cards created exclusively for students. These cards typically have smaller credit limits and can be an excellent place to start when building credit. Remember to use the card responsibly and make timely payments.

Responsible Credit Usage:

Using credit responsibly is crucial to avoid falling into debt and damaging your credit history. Here are some key points to keep in mind:

- Make On-Time Payments: To preserve a positive payment history, pay your credit card bills or loan installments on time. Late payments may incur late penalties and have a negative influence on your credit score.

- Reduce Credit usage: Credit usage is the percentage of available credit that you use. To maintain a healthy credit profile, keep your credit utilization below 30%.

- Be aware of interest rates and fees: Interest and fees are frequently assessed on credit cards and loans. It's critical to recognize these expenditures and budget for them.

- Review and comprehend credit agreements: Before accepting any credit offer, read and comprehend the terms and conditions thoroughly. Keep an eye out for interest rates, fees, and payback conditions.

- Keep an eye on your credit: Examine your credit report on a regular basis report to ensure its accuracy and detect any signs of identity theft or errors. You can obtain a free copy of your credit report once a year.

Always keep in mind that credit is a financial responsibility that must be managed wisely. Using credit properly can help you build a good credit history, which will help you in the future when applying for loans, renting apartments, or even finding work. However, it is critical to understand the dangers involved with credit and make prudent financial decisions that are in line with your financial objectives. If you have any questions or need help, don't be afraid to ask your parents, guardians, or trusted adults for advice based on their own experiences. Developing strong credit practices now will set you up for financial success later in life.

DEALING WITH DEBT

As you navigate the complexities of personal finance, one crucial aspect to understand is debt management. Debt refers to money borrowed from lenders or creditors that must be repaid over time. While debt can offer opportunities and flexibility, it is vital to manage it responsibly to avoid financial stress. Let's explore key strategies for effective debt management, providing you with valuable insights on how to stay in control of your financial well-being.

To begin, it is essential to gain a clear understanding of the debt you have accumulated. Take the time to compile a comprehensive list that includes the types of debt, outstanding balances, interest rates, and minimum monthly payments. This exercise will enable you to assess your overall financial situation and help you prioritize your repayment strategy effectively.

Developing a budget is a fundamental step in managing your debt. A budget allows you to track your income and expenses, providing insight into how much money you can allocate towards debt repayment each month. By creating a realistic budget and adhering to it, you can ensure that you have enough funds to meet your debt obligations while also addressing other financial needs.

If you find yourself burdened with multiple debts, it is crucial to prioritize those with higher interest rates. High-interest debts, such as credit card balances, can quickly accumulate and become more challenging to repay. Allocate more of your repayment budget towards these debts to pay them off faster and reduce the amount of interest you'll ultimately pay.

Timely payments are of utmost importance when managing your debt. Strive to make your debt payments on time to avoid late fees and penalties. Late payments can also have a negative impact on your credit score, affecting your ability to obtain credit in the future. Whenever possible, aim to pay more than the minimum amount due each month. By doing so, you can reduce the overall interest you will pay and accelerate the debt payoff process.

While managing your existing debt, it is crucial to resist the temptation of taking on new debt unless absolutely necessary. Take a close look at your spending habits and differentiate between wants and needs. Prioritize saving money and building an emergency fund to cover unexpected expenses, thereby reducing the likelihood of relying on credit in the future.

If you find yourself struggling to manage your debt or feeling overwhelmed, do not hesitate to seek professional guidance. Financial counselors or credit counseling agencies can provide valuable advice on debt management strategies, budgeting techniques, and negotiating with creditors. They can help you develop a personalized plan to regain control of your finances and provide the necessary support throughout your journey towards financial stability.

Managing debt can be challenging, but staying motivated is crucial. Set specific financial goals and celebrate milestones along the way. As you pay off debts, the feeling of financial freedom and reduced stress will serve as powerful motivation to continue your journey towards becoming debt-free.

Keep in mind that managing debt is a fundamental skill for achieving financial well-being. By understanding your debt, creating a budget, prioritizing high-interest debt, making timely payments, avoiding additional debt, seeking professional guidance when needed, and staying motivated, you can take control of your financial future. Remember, effective debt management requires discipline, commitment, and patience. By implementing these strategies early in life, you will develop sound financial habits and set yourself up for a more secure and prosperous future.

CHAPTER 5

BANKING AND FINANCIAL SERVICES

As a teenager entering the world of personal finance, understanding banking and financial services is crucial. One of the first steps in managing your money effectively is choosing the right bank account. In this chapter, we will explore the importance of banking, the various types of bank accounts available, and key considerations for selecting the right account to meet your financial needs.

Banking plays a central role in managing your finances. Banks provide a range of financial services that are essential for everyday life. They offer secure places to store your money, provide convenient payment options, and facilitate transactions such as receiving your salary, paying bills, or making purchases. Banks also offer additional services like loans, investment opportunities, and financial advice. Therefore, selecting the right bank and account is vital for a solid financial foundation.

When it comes to bank accounts, there are several options available. Let's explore the most common types of accounts suitable for teenagers:

- Savings Accounts:

A savings account is a basic account designed for accumulating and storing money. It typically offers a low or no minimum balance requirement and provides a modest interest rate on your deposited funds. Savings accounts are ideal for building an emergency fund, saving for short-term goals, and developing good savings habits.

- Checking Accounts:

A checking account is a transactional account that allows you to deposit and withdraw money easily. It provides features such as writing checks, making electronic transfers, and using a debit card for purchases. Checking accounts are suitable for managing everyday expenses and providing quick access to your funds.

- Student Accounts:

Many banks offer specialized accounts designed specifically for students. These accounts often come with benefits such as lower fees, higher withdrawal limits, and educational resources. Student accounts are suitable for teenagers who are studying and starting to manage their finances independently.

When selecting a bank account, there are several factors to consider, like;

Fees and Charges:

Different accounts may have varying fees associated with transactions, account maintenance, and minimum balance requirements. Look for accounts with low or no fees to minimize unnecessary costs.

Interest Rates:

If you're interested in earning interest on your savings, compare the interest rates offered by different banks. While interest rates for basic accounts may be relatively low, every bit of interest earned can contribute to your financial growth.

Convenience and Accessibility:

Consider the convenience and accessibility of the bank's branches, ATMs, and online/mobile banking services. Look for a bank that offers a wide network of ATMs, online banking features, and a user-friendly mobile app to manage your finances conveniently.

Customer Service and Support:

Pay attention to the quality of customer service provided by the bank. Look for institutions with a reputation for excellent customer support, as it can be helpful in addressing any questions or concerns you may have.

Educational Resources:

Some banks offer educational resources and financial literacy programs to help you develop your financial skills. These resources can be valuable in enhancing your understanding of banking, budgeting, and other financial topics.

Choosing the right bank account is an essential step in managing your finances effectively. By understanding the importance of banking, exploring the different types of accounts available, and considering factors such as fees, interest rates, convenience, customer service, and educational resources, you can make an informed decision that aligns with your financial goals as a teenager. Remember, selecting the right bank account is an important foundation for building good financial habits and establishing a solid financial future.

ONLINE BANKING AND MOBILE APPS

In today's digital age, technology has revolutionized the way we manage our finances. Online banking and mobile apps have made it easier than ever to access and control our money from the comfort of our smartphones or computers. As a teenager, understanding and utilizing these digital tools can provide convenience, security, and valuable financial management skills. There are numerous benefits that comes with online banking, let's explore few of them

• Convenience and Accessibility:

Online banking and mobile apps offer unparalleled convenience. You can access your bank account anytime, anywhere, eliminating the need to visit a physical branch. Whether you want to check your balance, view transaction history, transfer funds, or pay bills, these tools provide instant access to your financial information.

• Enhanced Financial Management:

These digital tools empower you to take control of your finances. You can track your expenses, categorize transactions, set budgeting goals, and receive notifications about account activity. With real-time updates, you gain a better understanding of your spending habits, allowing you to make more informed financial decisions.

• Speed and Efficiency:

Traditional banking transactions can take time, involving paperwork and waiting in line. Online banking and mobile apps expedite these processes. You can transfer funds between accounts, pay bills, and even deposit checks by simply taking a photo. This saves time and effort, allowing you to focus on other important aspects of your life.

• Enhanced Security Measures:

Many online banking platforms and mobile apps implement robust security measures to protect your financial information. These include encryption, multi-factor authentication, and biometric authentication (such as fingerprint or facial recognition). Additionally, you can set up alerts to notify you of any suspicious activity, ensuring the safety of your accounts.

Online banking and mobile app usage is opened to everyone, including you. To enjoy it's numerous benefits, you should;

- Choose a Reputable Bank:

Select a bank with a strong reputation for online banking and mobile app services. Research customer reviews and ratings to ensure they offer a user-friendly interface, advanced security features, and reliable customer support.

- Set Up Online Banking:

Visit your bank's website and follow the instructions to enroll in online banking. This typically involves creating a username and password. Make sure your password is strong, unique and not easily guessable by others, also ensure you choose a password that you can remember easily.

- Download the Mobile App:

Once you have enrolled in online banking, download your bank's mobile app from your smartphone's app store. Install the app and log in using your online banking credentials. Ensure that you only download the official app provided by your bank to ensure security.

- Explore Features and Functions:

Take the time to explore the various features and functions available in the online banking platform and mobile app. Familiarize yourself with options such as checking account balances, reviewing transaction history, transferring funds, setting up bill payments, and managing alerts. Some apps may also provide tools for budgeting and financial goal setting.

•Practice Good Security Habits:

To ensure the security of your online banking and mobile app, follow best practices such as:

 - Regularly update your app and operating system to benefit from the latest security enhancements.

 - Avoid accessing your accounts on public Wi-Fi networks, as they may be vulnerable to hackers.

 - Use strong and unique passwords, and consider enabling biometric authentication if available.

 - Be cautious of phishing attempts and only enter your login credentials on official banking websites or mobile apps.

In conclusion, online banking and mobile apps offer tremendous benefits for managing your finances as a teenager. With convenience, enhanced financial management capabilities, speed, and security features, these tools empower you to take control of your money and develop valuable financial skills. By choosing a reputable bank, setting up online banking, downloading the official mobile app, exploring features, and practicing good security habits, you can make the most of these digital tools and embark on a journey towards financial empowerment.

Embrace the digital age of banking and enjoy the convenience it brings to your financial life

LOAN AND MORTGAGE

It's crucial to have a firm grasp of loans as you navigate the realm of personal finance. Loans are financial instruments that enable people to borrow money for certain needs, such as paying for a car, financing college, or handling unforeseen costs. The fundamentals of loans, their varieties, and important factors for responsible borrowing will all be covered in this section

Let's Explore the different types of Loan

1. Personal Loans: Personal loans are all-purpose loans that can be utilized for a variety of purposes, such as debt consolidation, vacation finance, or paying for medical costs. They frequently don't need collateral because they are unsecured loans. The periods of personal loans can range from a few months to several years, and the interest rates may be fixed or variable.

2. Student Loans: Student loans can be used to pay for living expenses, tuition, and other expenditures associated with higher education. They might be acquired through public or private lending initiatives. Low interest rates and flexible repayment choices are common features of student loans. Before taking out student loans, it's vital to do some research, evaluate the various loan possibilities, and comprehend the terms and circumstances.

3. Auto Loans: Auto loans are made expressly to pay for a car. These loans are secured by the vehicle itself, which means that if the borrower defaults on the loan, the automobile may be repossessed. Auto loans typically feature set interest rates and durations of two to seven years for repayment. Compare interest rates, loan periods, required down payments, and the affordability of the monthly payment when choosing a vehicle loan.

There are obligations associated with taking out loans. Here are some crucial things to remember:

1. Identify Your Needs: Before applying for a loan, evaluate your financial status and decide what you need the money for specifically. Only borrow what you actually need and can afford to repay.

2. Investigate and Compare: Spend some time investigating various loan providers. Examine interest rates, repayment schedules, costs, and any other important considerations. Select a dependable lender that offers cost-effective terms that support your financial objectives.

3. Recognize the Terms: Carefully read the loan agreement and ensure that you comprehend all of the terms and conditions, including interest rates, repayment plans, fees, and any penalties for making payments late or repaying the loan early.

4. Create a budget to make sure you can return your loan on time without hurting your finances. Make loan payments a priority to prevent late fees and damage to your credit score.

5. **Establish and Maintain excellent Credit:** It's critical to cultivate excellent credit habits, such as timely bill payment and responsible credit use. You can get future loans with good terms if you have a solid credit history.

When used carefully and for the correct purposes, loans can help with finances. Effective loan management requires knowing the various loan types that are available, investigating and comparing lenders, and borrowing responsibly. Always proceed with prudence while borrowing, keeping in mind your ability to pay it back and the long-term financial consequences. Loans can be useful tools in helping you achieve your financial objectives if you have the right information and use safe borrowing techniques.

MORTGAGE

It's crucial to educate yourself about the idea of mortgages as you set out on your path to financial independence. A mortgage is a type of loan made especially to assist people in buying a home. Although it is a big financial commitment, you may make judgments concerning homeownership provided you are properly informed. The fundamentals of mortgages, their essential elements, and significant factors for teens will all be covered in this section

A mortgage is a loan given to you by a financial entity, like a bank or mortgage lender, in order to assist you in financing the purchase of a home. It is a commitment that lasts for a considerable amount of time—typically 15 to 30 years—during which you make consistent payments to pay back the loan and interest.

Check out the Important Elements of a Mortgage

Principal: The initial sum you borrow from the lender to buy your house is referred to as the principal. It is equal to the total cost of the property less the down payment.

Interest Rate: The cost of borrowing money from a lender is represented by the interest rate. It impacts the total amount you will pay back over the course of the mortgage and is indicated as a percentage of the loan amount. It is possible for interest rates to be either fixed (stay the same for the duration of the loan) or adjustable (alter periodically in response to market conditions).

Down payment: The down payment is an advance payment that represents a portion of the home's buying price. It lowers the mortgage loan's balance. Saving money for a down payment is a crucial step since it shows that you are committed to becoming a homeowner and because it can have an impact on your interest rate and monthly mortgage payments.

Loan Term: The period of time over which you will repay the mortgage is referred to as the loan term. Typically, it is 15, 20, or 30 years. Longer loan terms result in lower monthly payments but greater interest throughout the course of the loan, whereas shorter loan terms result in higher monthly payments but less overall interest paid.

Monthly Payments: Principal and interest are both included in your monthly mortgage payments. They frequently also contain extra sums for homeowner's insurance and real estate taxes, which the lender holds in an escrow account and pays on your behalf.

Here are important things to think about when planning to take a mortgage

Affordability: Carefully evaluate your financial status and decide what you can comfortably afford before applying for a mortgage. Take into account not only the monthly mortgage payment but also additional homeownership expenses like utilities, insurance, property taxes, and upkeep fees.

Creditworthiness: Before approving a mortgage, lenders check your creditworthiness. You may increase your chances of getting a suitable mortgage offer by developing and keeping solid credit habits including timely bill payment, responsible debt management, and refraining from taking on too much new credit.

Investigation and comparison: Spend some time investigating and contrasting mortgage lenders. Look for reasonable loan terms, low interest rates, and dependable customer service. You can get the finest mortgage choice for your needs by doing some comparison shopping.

Other charges: In addition to the down payment and mortgage payments, you should be aware of any additional charges related to purchasing a home, such as closing costs (fees for loan processing, appraisals, and title insurance), moving costs, and potential property repairs or upgrades.

Long-Term Financial Planning: Purchasing a property entails significant financial responsibilities. When considering whether to take out a mortgage, take into account your financial security, lifestyle goals, and professional aspirations. Making ensuring homeownership fits into your entire financial objectives is crucial.

To be able to own a home, you must make a sizeable financial commitment known as a mortgage. For teenagers interested in seeking a mortgage, it is essential to understand its important components, carefully examine affordability, maintain good credit, perform research, and take long-term financial planning into account. Owning a home can be gratifying, you may start this exciting road toward house ownership with experience, smart decision-making, and complete comprehension.

To negotiate the complexity of mortgages and make wise decisions, always seek advice from trusted adults or experts, such as financial consultants or mortgage specialists.

CHAPTER 6

MAKING MONEY

As a teenager, you may be eager to start earning your own money and become financially independent. It's an exciting step towards taking control of your finances and building a solid foundation for your future. In this chapter, we will explore various ways you can make money as a teenager, and tips for success.

Making money as a teenager can be a rewarding experience that teaches you valuable life skills and financial responsibility. By exploring various earning opportunities, setting financial goals, budgeting, saving, and continuously learning about personal finance, you can establish a strong financial foundation for your future.

PART-TIME JOBS

As a teenager, part-time jobs can offer you a wealth of benefits beyond just earning money. They provide valuable experiences, teach important life skills, and help you prepare for your future. In this guide, we will explore the importance of part-time jobs, how to find one, and tips for successfully managing your responsibilities.

Part-time jobs give you the opportunity to earn your own money and become financially independent. You can use your earnings to save for future goals, contribute to your expenses, or learn the value of money through responsible spending.

Part-time jobs provide a platform to develop and enhance essential skills that will benefit you in various aspects of life. These skills include time management, communication, teamwork, problem-solving, customer service, and responsibility. Such skills are transferable and highly valued by employers.

Part-time jobs offer a chance to gain practical work experience, even at a young age. This experience can be added to your resume and will make you stand out when applying for future jobs or internships.

Interacting with colleagues, supervisors, and customers in a part-time job setting allows you to expand your network and build professional connections. These connections may prove valuable in the future when seeking employment or exploring career opportunities.

To find a part-time job that suit you, you should consider your passions, hobbies, and skills to help guide your job search. Look for opportunities that align with your interests, as this will increase job satisfaction. Then you should visit local businesses such as retail stores, restaurants, movie theaters, or cafes, and inquire about part-time job openings. Many businesses often advertise vacancies through signs or online job boards.

You can as well use online platforms like job search websites or social media groups to find part-time job opportunities. Websites like Indeed, Snagajob, or local job boards can be great resources for finding openings in your area.

You should also inform your family, friends, and neighbors that you are searching for a part-time job. They may have connections or be aware of job opportunities that are not widely advertised.

Managing Your Part-Time Job effectively and balancing it with you academic work should be put in consideration. To do this effectively, you need to;

- Prioritize Time Management:

Balance your part-time job with your academic commitments and other activities. Create a schedule that allows you to allocate time effectively, ensuring you can fulfill your responsibilities without neglecting other important aspects of your life.

- Communicate and Be Reliable:

Demonstrate professionalism and reliability by being punctual, following instructions, and communicating effectively with your supervisors and coworkers. Clear communication helps establish a positive work environment and fosters good relationships with your colleagues.

- Learn and Grow:

Approach your part-time job with a growth mindset. Take the opportunity to learn from your experiences, seek feedback, and strive for continuous improvement. Embrace challenges and view them as opportunities for personal and professional growth.

- Practice Responsibility:

Take ownership of your job responsibilities, complete tasks diligently, and fulfill your commitments. Show initiative and a strong work ethic, as these qualities are highly valued in the workplace.

FREELANCING AND GIG ECONOMY

In today's ever-evolving job market, freelancing and the gig economy offer exciting opportunities for teenagers to explore flexible work arrangements and develop valuable skills. Whether you have a specific talent or are interested in trying out different tasks, freelancing and gig work can provide financial independence and valuable experiences. Let's explore the world of freelancing and the gig economy, its benefits, and how to get started.

Freelancing involves offering your services or skills to clients or companies on a project basis. As a freelancer, you are self-employed and typically work with multiple clients simultaneously. Common freelance areas include writing, graphic design, programming, social media management, tutoring, and more. Freelancers often set their own rates, determine their working hours, and enjoy the flexibility of choosing projects that align with their interests and skills.

The gig economy refers to a labor market characterized by short-term, flexible, and often on-demand work. It involves completing individual tasks or "gigs" rather than having a traditional full-time job. Platforms like Uber, TaskRabbit, Upwork, and Fiverr connect individuals with gig opportunities across various industries. Gigs can range from driving passengers to delivering groceries, running errands, or providing virtual assistance. The gig economy allows individuals to work when they want, giving them more control over their schedules.

Benefits of Freelancing and the Gig Economy

Flexibility

Freelancing and gig work offer flexibility in terms of working hours and location. You can choose when and where you work, allowing you to balance work with other commitments such as school, hobbies, or personal pursuits.

Skill Development

Engaging in freelancing or gig work exposes you to diverse projects and tasks. This enables you to develop a wide range of skills, such as communication, time management, adaptability, and problem-solving. As you take on different gigs, you'll gain valuable experience and expand your skill set.

Financial Independence

Freelancing and gig work provide an opportunity to earn money and gain financial independence. You have control over your earning potential, and your income can be directly influenced by your effort, skills, and the number of gigs you take on.

To get started,

1. Identify Your Skills and Interests:

Consider your talents, passions, and areas of expertise. Determine what services or tasks you can offer as a freelancer or gig worker. This could be anything from writing, graphic design, web development, photography, virtual assistance, or even delivering goods.

2. Create an Online Presence:

Build a professional online presence by creating profiles on freelancing platforms or gig economy apps. Showcase your skills, previous work samples, and qualifications. A strong online presence will help attract potential clients or gig opportunities.

3. Network and Seek Referrals:

Inform your friends, family, and acquaintances about your freelance or gig work. They might know someone who needs your services or can refer you to potential clients. Networking is a powerful way to expand your professional connections and gain new opportunities.

4. Market Yourself:

Promote your services by creating a portfolio or website. Use social media platforms to showcase your work and reach a wider audience. Actively engage with relevant communities or groups where potential clients or employers might be present.

5. Provide Excellent Service:

Deliver high-quality work and provide exceptional customer service to build a strong reputation. Positive client feedback and referrals can significantly boost your freelancing or gig career.

Exploring freelancing and the gig economy as a teenager can be an exciting and rewarding endeavor. It offers flexibility, skill development, and financial independence. By identifying your skills, building a strong online presence, networking, and delivering excellent service, you can embark on a successful freelancing or gig career. Remember to continuously learn and adapt to the changing demands of the market, and enjoy the opportunities that come your way.

ENTREPRENEURSHIP

Entrepreneurship offers a world of possibilities for teenagers who are eager to turn their ideas into reality, make a positive impact, and create their own path. It allows you to take control of your future, embrace innovation, and develop valuable skills along the way. In this section, we will explore the exciting world of entrepreneurship, its benefits, and how to embark on this journey with confidence.

Entrepreneurship is the process of identifying opportunities, taking risks, and creating a business or organization to meet a need or solve a problem. It involves bringing together resources, ideas, and talent to develop products, services, or solutions that provide value to customers or society. Entrepreneurs are driven by a passion for their vision, a willingness to take risks, and a desire to make a difference. Remember the story of Alex, shared a few chapters back, that's entrepreneurship.

Entrepreneurship allows you to be your own boss and create something unique. You have the freedom to explore your passions, pursue innovative ideas, and shape your own destiny.

As an entrepreneur, you will constantly be learning and growing. You will develop a wide range of skills, such as critical thinking, problem-solving, leadership, communication, and adaptability. Entrepreneurship provides opportunities for personal and professional development like no other path.

Entrepreneurs have the power to make a positive impact on society. By addressing unmet needs or solving problems, you can create products or services that improve people's lives, contribute to sustainability, or drive social change.

To become a successful entrepreneur, Start by identifying your passions, interests, and the problems you want to solve. Consider what motivates you and aligns with your values. This will form the foundation of your entrepreneurial journey.

Look for problems or needs within your community or areas that interest you. Brainstorm potential solutions or innovations that can address those issues. Conduct market research to validate your ideas and understand your target audience.

Now, you can create a comprehensive business plan that outlines your vision, mission, target market, competition, marketing strategies, financial projections, and operational details. A business plan helps you stay focused and provides a roadmap for your entrepreneurial journey.

You should also connect with experienced entrepreneurs or professionals who can provide mentorship and guidance. They can offer insights, share their experiences, and help you navigate the challenges of starting a business.

Networking is crucial for entrepreneurs, attend events, join entrepreneurial organizations or clubs, and connect with like-minded individuals. Build relationships with potential customers, partners, and mentors who can support and contribute to your success.

Entrepreneurship is a journey filled with ups and downs. Embrace challenges, learn from failures, and maintain a growth mindset. Be open to feedback, adapt to changes, and continuously seek opportunities for learning and improvement. Begin by taking small steps towards your entrepreneurial goals. Launch a minimum viable product or offer your services on a smaller scale to test the market and gather feedback. Taking action is key to turning your ideas into reality.

Familiarize yourself with marketing strategies to effectively reach your target audience and promote your products or services.

Entrepreneurship requires persistence and resilience. Be prepared for setbacks and challenges along the way. Stay focused on your goals, learn from failures, and adapt your approach. Perseverance is often the key to long-term success.

Embarking on an entrepreneurial journey as a teenager is an exciting and rewarding endeavor. By identifying your passions, exploring ideas, seeking mentorship, building a network, and taking action, you can bring your entrepreneurial dreams to life. Embrace challenges, stay persistent, and never stop learning.

Remember, entrepreneurship is a continuous learning process. Embrace the opportunities for growth and the chance to make a positive impact. With determination, creativity, and a commitment to your vision, you can become a successful and fulfilled entrepreneur.

Wishing you a thrilling and transformative journey in entrepreneurship

CHAPTER 7

CASE STUDIES AND REAL-LIFE EXAMPLES

Case Study 1

The story of Elon Musk is a remarkable example of someone who started with humble beginnings and went on to achieve extraordinary financial success. Born in Pretoria, South Africa, in 1971, Musk faced a challenging childhood but possessed a relentless drive and an insatiable curiosity that would shape his future.

At a young age, Musk developed a deep fascination with computers and technology. In 1984, at the age of 12, he sold his first software, a BASIC-based video game called Blastar, for $500. This early entrepreneurial venture revealed his innate talent for innovation and his desire to create and sell products.

After completing high school, Musk left South Africa to attend the University of Pennsylvania in the United States. He earned dual bachelor's degrees in physics and economics, setting the stage for his future endeavors. Musk then pursued a Ph.D. at Stanford University but dropped out after just two days to embark on his entrepreneurial journey.

In the late 1990s, Musk co-founded Zip2, a software company that developed online business directories and maps for newspapers.

Despite facing numerous setbacks and financial difficulties, Musk persevered, eventually selling Zip2 to Compaq for approximately $300 million.

This early success laid the foundation for Musk's ambitious vision. In 2002, he co-founded SpaceX, a private aerospace manufacturer and space transportation company. Musk's goal was to revolutionize space exploration and make humanity a multi-planetary species. SpaceX faced multiple failures and near bankruptcy but ultimately succeeded in becoming the first privately-funded company to launch and recover a spacecraft.

While SpaceX pursued the stars, Musk also set his sights on transforming the automotive industry. In 2004, he became the chairman and largest shareholder of Tesla Motors (now Tesla, Inc.), an electric vehicle company. Despite skepticism from industry experts, Musk led Tesla through numerous challenges and setbacks, including production delays and financial difficulties. Today, Tesla is one of the world's most valuable car companies, producing electric vehicles that have revolutionized the industry.

Musk's entrepreneurial journey did not stop there. He also co-founded SolarCity (now part of Tesla), a solar energy services company, and Neuralink, a neurotechnology company focused on developing brain-computer interfaces. Additionally, he took on the challenge of revolutionizing transportation with The Boring Company, which aims to create an underground tunnel network for efficient transportation systems.

Musk's relentless pursuit of his visions and his ability to innovate and disrupt multiple industries have propelled him to immense financial success. As of 2021, he is one of the richest individuals in the world.

Elon Musk's story is an inspiring testament to the power of determination, resilience, and unwavering belief in one's ideas. From selling video games as a teenager to becoming a visionary entrepreneur and influential figure, his journey serves as a reminder that with passion, hard work, and a relentless drive, anyone can overcome obstacles and achieve extraordinary success.

Case Study 2

Here is the story of Maya, the girl who rose as a freelancer. Maya had always possessed a passion for writing and a gift for storytelling. Inspired by her love for words, she set out on a journey to pursue a career as a freelance writer.

With a laptop as her most prized possession, Maya embarked on her freelancing adventure. She spent countless hours honing her writing skills, researching various industries, and crafting captivating content. Despite facing initial challenges and rejections, Maya remained determined to turn her passion into a thriving career.

As Maya continued to refine her craft, she discovered online platforms that connected freelancers with clients from all over the world. She eagerly created her profile and started bidding on writing projects that aligned with her interests and expertise.

In the beginning, the projects were small, but Maya poured her heart and soul into each one, ensuring that her work exceeded expectations. Word of her exceptional talent spread among clients, and soon she found herself inundated with offers for writing assignments.

With her reputation growing, Maya expanded her skills to offer a broader range of services. She dabbled in copywriting, blog writing, content marketing, and even ventured into social media management. Her ability to adapt and evolve made her an invaluable asset to clients seeking creative solutions.

As Maya gained experience and built a strong client base, she started increasing her rates. Clients were willing to pay a premium for her top-notch work, recognizing the value she brought to their businesses. Maya began to earn a comfortable income, allowing her to enjoy financial stability while doing what she loved most.

One of the key advantages of freelancing for Maya was the flexibility it offered. She could work from anywhere, setting her own schedule and choosing projects that aligned with her interests. This freedom allowed her to maintain a healthy work-life balance and pursue personal endeavors alongside her thriving freelance career.

As Maya's reputation soared, she started receiving invitations to collaborate on larger projects and with renowned companies in her industry. Her name became synonymous with excellence and creativity. She seized these opportunities, pushing herself beyond her comfort zone and embracing new challenges.

Maya's success as a freelancer was not only defined by financial achievements but also by the personal fulfillment it brought her. She realized that freelancing allowed her to leverage her passion, talents, and skills while making a significant impact on her clients' businesses. Maya felt a sense of pride knowing that her work contributed to their success and growth.

With time, Maya's freelancing journey led her to start her own agency, where she could mentor and collaborate with other talented freelancers. She created a supportive community that fostered creativity, collaboration, and continuous growth. Maya's agency thrived, becoming a hub of innovative ideas and successful projects.

Maya's story serves as a testament to the power of freelancing. Through her dedication, perseverance, and unwavering passion for her craft, she transformed her talent into a flourishing and fulfilling career. Her journey demonstrates that with the right skills, determination, and a commitment to excellence, anyone can achieve financial success and personal fulfillment through freelancing.

Always remember Maya's story as you embark on your own freelancing journey. Embrace your unique talents, continually refine your skills, and pursue your passion with unwavering dedication. With each project, you bring your dreams closer to reality, forging a path to financial success and personal fulfillment in the exciting world of freelancing.

Case Study 3

Here is the inspiring story of Sara Blakely, an entrepreneur who achieved remarkable financial success.

Sara Blakely, born in Clearwater, Florida, had always possessed an entrepreneurial spirit and a knack for spotting opportunities. After completing her education, she worked various odd jobs while searching for her true calling. Little did she know that her journey would lead her to create a billion-dollar business.

One day, Sara had a fashion dilemma. She wanted to wear a pair of white pants but struggled to find suitable undergarments that would remain invisible beneath them. Determined to find a solution, she took matters into her own hands and used her creative thinking to invent a game-changing product.

Armed with a sewing machine and her ingenuity, Sara designed a comfortable, lightweight undergarment that provided a smooth, seamless look. She named her invention "Spanx." Recognizing the potential of her innovative product, Sara decided to turn her idea into a business.

With her life savings of $5,000, Sara embarked on her entrepreneurial journey. She faced numerous challenges, including convincing manufacturers to produce her product and convincing retailers to stock it on their shelves. However, Sara's unwavering belief in the power of her invention kept her moving forward.

Persistence paid off, and Spanx started gaining traction. The product resonated with women around the world who sought confidence and comfort in their attire. Through word-of-mouth and positive reviews, Spanx began to dominate the market, revolutionizing the shapewear industry.

Sara's entrepreneurial spirit and dedication catapulted her to financial success. She quickly became the youngest self-made female billionaire, and her company, Spanx, continued to flourish. However, Sara's success went beyond financial gains.

With her newfound wealth, Sara established the Sara Blakely Foundation, focusing on empowering women through education, entrepreneurship, and support. She became an influential advocate for female entrepreneurs, sharing her knowledge and experiences to inspire others to pursue their dreams.

Sara's story embodies the power of determination, resilience, and a keen eye for opportunities. She transformed a simple idea into a multi-billion-dollar business, all while empowering women and making a positive impact on their lives. Sara's journey exemplifies that anyone, with the right mindset and unwavering determination, can achieve extraordinary financial success while making a difference in the world.

So, dear teen, let Sara Blakely's story inspire you to embrace your own entrepreneurial aspirations. With creativity, perseverance, and a belief in your ideas, you have the potential to create something extraordinary. Dream big, work hard, and let the world be your canvas as you embark on your own path to financial success and making a meaningful impact.

CASE STUDY 4

I met Lily a few years back, here is her story into financial freedom. From a young age, Lily had a natural flair for identifying opportunities and turning them into profitable ventures.

At the age of 14, Lily found herself in need of some extra spending money. She brainstormed different ways to earn money while leveraging her skills and interests. Inspired by her love for baking, Lily decided to start a small home-based bakery.

Equipped with her mother's recipes and her own creative twists, Lily took a loan from her mother and began baking delicious cookies, cupcakes, and other sweet treats. She carefully packaged her goodies and started selling them to friends, family, and neighbors. The response was overwhelming, with everyone raving about the quality and taste of her baked goods.

Word of mouth spread, and Lily's little bakery gained popularity within the community. Encouraged by the positive feedback and growing demand, she decided to expand her business. Lily got a relative to created a simple website for her business, with this, she started taking online orders, catering to special events, parties, and local businesses.

With her earnings, Lily reinvested in her business, purchasing quality ingredients and upgrading her baking equipment. She attended workshops and classes to further develop her baking skills, constantly striving to deliver exceptional products to her customers.

As her reputation grew, Lily began experimenting with new recipes and innovative flavors. She carefully curated seasonal menus and introduced unique custom-designed cakes. Her attention to detail and dedication to customer satisfaction set her apart from competitors.

Lily's entrepreneurial success wasn't limited to her bakery alone. She recognized the power of social media and utilized platforms like Instagram and Facebook to showcase her creations, attract new customers, and engage with her audience. Her online presence expanded her reach beyond the local community, attracting customers from neighboring towns and even different states.

With her earnings, Lily developed a habit of saving and investing. She learned about personal finance, sought advice from mentors, and explored different investment opportunities. Lily understood the importance of not only making money but also managing and growing it wisely.

By the time Lily graduated from high school, her bakery had become a flourishing business. She had accumulated significant savings and even expanded her operations by opening a small storefront. Lily's success as a teenage entrepreneur inspired many others in her community, who admired her dedication, perseverance, and business acumen.

Lily's entrepreneurial journey taught her invaluable life lessons. She learned the importance of passion, perseverance, and continuous learning. Through her entrepreneurial endeavors, Lily discovered her strengths, honed her skills, and gained confidence in her abilities.

But perhaps the most significant aspect of Lily's story was the empowerment she felt as a young person taking control of her financial future. She realized that age was not a barrier to success and that with determination, creativity, and a strong work ethic, anyone could achieve their dreams, regardless of their age.

So, dear teenager, let Lily's story inspire you to explore your passions and talents. Don't be afraid to think outside the box, take risks, and turn your ideas into reality. Whether it's starting a small business, freelancing, or pursuing your creative passions, seize the opportunities that come your way and embrace the entrepreneurial spirit within you. Who knows? You might just uncover your own path to financial success at a young age, just like Lily did.

Case Study 5

At about the time I met Lily, I also met this young man named Lucas, here is his story.

Lucas, as at when I met him was in his mid twenties, he had always been responsible with his finances. He worked diligently and saved his money diligently, always planning for a secure future. However, even the most careful individuals can make mistakes, and Lucas was about to learn this lesson firsthand.

Lucas had been saving for years to purchase his dream car. He had diligently set aside money from his part-time job and resisted the temptation to spend it on other things. Finally, the day came when Lucas had saved enough to buy the car he had always desired.

Filled with excitement and anticipation, Lucas headed to the car dealership. As he browsed through the shiny vehicles, a salesman approached him and introduced him to a newer, more expensive model. The salesman emphasized the car's features and its potential for resale value, convincing Lucas that it was a wise investment.

Caught up in the moment and influenced by the persuasive sales pitch, Lucas made a hasty decision. He opted for the more expensive car, financing it with a loan that required higher monthly payments. Lucas believed he had made a smart choice, thinking that the car's resale value would offset the higher costs.

However, things didn't go as planned. The car's resale value depreciated faster than Lucas had anticipated. Additionally, the monthly payments were more burdensome than he had expected, leaving him with little room to save or invest. Lucas found himself struggling to make ends meet, sacrificing other financial goals and experiencing constant stress.

Lucas had learned a valuable lesson about the consequences of impulsive decisions and failing to carefully consider the long-term implications. He realized that he had let the allure of instant gratification cloud his judgment, and it had cost him dearly.

But Lucas didn't let this mistake define him. Instead, he chose to learn from it and take control of his financial future. He educated himself about personal finance, budgeting, and making informed decisions. Lucas developed a plan to pay off his debt as quickly as possible, cutting back on unnecessary expenses and exploring ways to increase his income.

Through discipline and perseverance, Lucas successfully paid off his car loan and regained his financial footing. He rebuilt his savings, this time with a focus on emergency funds and long-term investments. Lucas vowed never to repeat the same mistake and became a beacon of financial wisdom among his peers.

Lucas's story serves as a reminder that anyone can make mistakes, especially when it comes to finances. It's important to approach financial decisions with caution, thoroughly research options, and weigh the long-term consequences. By learning from our mistakes and taking proactive steps to rectify them, we can regain control of our finances and build a more secure future.

Let Lucas's story be a lesson in financial prudence. Take the time to analyze your choices, seek advice from trusted sources, and consider the long-term impact of your decisions. Remember, financial mistakes are opportunities for growth and learning. Embrace them, make amends, and pave the way for a brighter financial future.

CONCLUSION

In conclusion, this book has aimed to provide valuable knowledge and guidance to teenagers on various aspects of personal finance, entrepreneurship, and financial success. We have explored the importance of budgeting, saving, and investing, as well as the significance of making wise financial decisions.

Throughout this journey, we have discovered that financial literacy and responsible money management are essential skills that can empower teenagers to take control of their financial futures. By understanding the concepts of income, expenses, savings, and investment, teenagers can develop a solid foundation for financial stability and growth.

We have delved into the world of part-time jobs, freelancing, and the gig economy, highlighting the opportunities available for teenagers to earn money and gain valuable skills. We have explored the world of entrepreneurship, inspiring young minds to embrace their passions, take risks, and create their own paths to success.

Additionally, we have discussed the importance of managing debt responsibly, making informed decisions about loans and mortgages, and understanding the role of credit in financial well-being. We have emphasized the significance of choosing the right bank account, utilizing online banking and mobile apps, and making the most of financial services available to teenagers.

Throughout this book, we have encountered stories of real-life individuals who have faced challenges, made mistakes, and ultimately achieved financial success through determination, perseverance, and a commitment to personal growth. These stories serve as reminders that anyone can achieve their goals with the right mindset, discipline, and a willingness to learn from their experiences.

As teenagers, you have the incredible opportunity to shape your financial destinies. By embracing the knowledge shared in this book and applying it to your own lives, you can set yourselves up for a future of financial independence, stability, and success.

Remember, financial success is not measured solely by wealth or possessions but also by your ability to make smart financial decisions, pursue your passions, and contribute to the well-being of others. By taking control of your financial journey today, you can build a solid foundation for a bright and prosperous future.

As you turn the final page of this book, remember that financial literacy is a lifelong learning process. Stay curious, continue to educate yourselves, and seek opportunities to grow your financial knowledge and skills. With determination, perseverance, and a commitment to personal growth, you can navigate the complexities of the financial world and build a life of financial well-being and fulfillment.

Now, it is time for you to embark on your own financial journey. Embrace the knowledge you have gained, make informed decisions, and seize the opportunities that come your way. May you find joy and fulfillment in managing your finances, pursuing your dreams, and creating a future filled with financial success and personal happiness.

Good luck on your financial journey, and may you always strive for prosperity and fulfillment in all aspects of your lives.